THE VALUE OF SELF-DISCIPLINE
The Story of Alexander Graham Bell

VALUE COMMUNICATIONS, INC.
PUBLISHERS
LA JOLLA, CALIFORNIA

THE VALUE OF SELF-DISCIPLINE

The Story of
Alexander Graham Bell

BY ANN DONEGAN JOHNSON

First Edition
Manufactured in the United States of America.
For information write to: ValueTales,
9601 Arrow Drive, San Diego, CA 92123

All dialogue in the text is fictitious.

Library of Congress Cataloging in Publication Data

Johnson, Ann Donegan.
    The value of self-discipline.

    (ValueTales)
    Originally published: The value of discipline.
LaJolla, Calif.: Value Communications,©1984.

    SUMMARY: Describes the boyhood and career of the
inventor of the telephone and teacher of the deaf,
emphasizing the importance of discipline in his life.
    1. Bell, Alexander Graham, 1847–1922—Juvenile
literature.   2. Discipline—Juvenile literature.
[1. Bell, Alexander Graham, 1847–1922. 2. Inventors.
3. Discipline] I. Pileggi, Steve, ill. II. Title.
III. Series.
TK6143.B4J64 1985   621.385'092'4 [B] [92]   85-7986
ISBN 0-7172-8176-0

V 85

This tale is about Alexander Graham Bell,
a man whose self-discipline and concern for
others led to some of the greatest inventions
of his time. The story that follows is based
on the events in his life. More historical
facts about Alexander Graham Bell can be
found on page 63.

Once upon a time...

in Edinburgh, Scotland, there lived a young boy named Alexander Graham Bell. His family called him Alec, and he was a very thoughtful little boy.

When Alec's father took him and his brothers for a walk up the hill overlooking the city, Alec would ask many questions.

"What kind of flower is that, father? How can birds fly without flapping their wings? What happens to butterflies in winter?"

Mr. Bell laughed. "So many questions, Alec. You'll have to give me time to answer them." Then he would answer Alec's questions one by one.

One day Mr. Bell took Alec to visit a mill where wheat was ground into flour to make bread. As usual Alec was full of questions.

"How do you get the hard outside husks off the grain?" Alec asked the mill owner.

"Ah, that's a problem," the mill owner replied. "It takes a long time to get rid of the husks. What we really need is a new tool to help us."

That night, as Alec was washing his hands, he had an idea.

"Maybe the mill owner could brush the husks off the grain like I brush dirt from my fingernails," he thought.

Alec was very pleased with his idea at first. Then it occurred to him that brushing husks off kernels one by one would take far too long. It was hard enough trying to get his nails clean.

Later, lying in bed, Alec thought and thought about the problem. Nothing he thought of seemed very good. He was feeling drowsy and discouraged when all of a sudden he thought he heard a voice. "That's a very interesting invention you are working on Alec," the voice said.

Startled, Alec opened his eyes. A little bell was floating in the air above his head. "Who are you?" Alec exclaimed. "Where did you come from, and since when do bells speak?"

"I'm Belle," announced this strange little creature. "I have decided to be your friend and give you encouragement when you need it. All inventors need lots of encouragement."

"Thank you," said Alec smiling. He was very proud to be thought of as an inventor. "My father is an inventor," he went on. "He is inventing a way to teach deaf people how to speak. I want to be like him when I grow up."

"You will, Alec," said his new friend. "You have at least one of the things it takes to become an inventor—a searching mind. It takes self-discipline too, of course. Lots of self-discipline. You may have to work on that. But I'll help you."

Being an honest little boy, Alec felt he had better tell Belle the whole truth. "My invention doesn't work, though."

"Not yet. But you can improve it if you try hard enough. Keep looking around you. The world is full of ideas, but you have to discipline your mind to search them out."

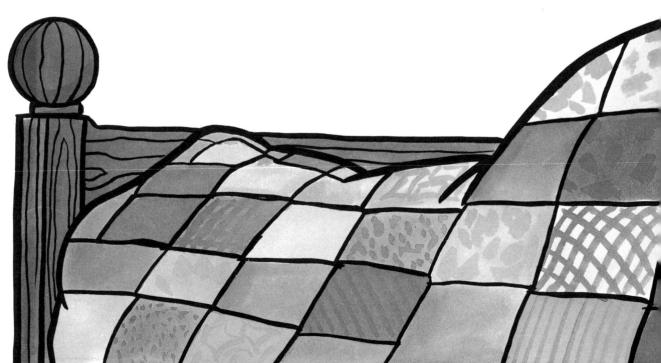

The next day Alec visited the mill with his father again and looked carefully at everything. He spotted a barrel-like machine that had paddles inside and a handle that turned it.

"That's it!" he shouted. He was so excited that at first the workers couldn't understand what he was talking about. When he had calmed down enough to make himself clear, they talked it over.

"Hmmm . . . brushes instead of paddles . . . it might work," one said. "They could pass over lots of grain again and again," added another. "It's worth a try," they agreed.

So they tried it . . . and it worked! Belle was right. If he disciplined himself to work on a problem, he could solve it.

From that day on Alec was forever thinking up new inventions and trying them out.

Belle was usually right there with him, very excited when things went well, encouraging Alec when things went wrong.

"Don't give up, Alec. Keep looking. It takes lots of self-discipline, but the answer is there somewhere."

Of course Alec knew that Belle wasn't real. He knew that when he heard the bell talk he was really hearing his own thoughts. But it was fun pretending that he had such a good friend. "After all," he said to himself, "inventing can be lonely work. I need someone to talk to and encourage me."

Mr. and Mrs. Bell were proud of their inventive son. But they were a little worried too.

"I had hoped he might become a pianist," said Mrs. Bell one night when Alec was fifteen. "He showed such talent when I was teaching him. But he seems to have lost interest."

"I know," agreed her husband. "His only interest seems to be inventing. I feel his school work may be suffering too."

"He's so bright, though. And he wants to learn and know about things," added Mrs. Bell. They both thought for a while. Suddenly Mrs. Bell exclaimed. "I think I have the answer! Why don't we send him to Grandfather Bell?"

"Of course! Now why didn't I think of that? He's enthusiastic but very disciplined—and an excellent teacher. Just what Alec needs!"

So Alec went to London to live and study with his grandfather for a year. The first day, Grandfather Bell took Alec into his library. There were so many books on the shelves that Alec could hardly see the walls.

"There's a lot of learning in this room, Alec," said Grandfather Bell. He picked up a book and held it out. "Why don't you start with this?"

"Have you read all these books?" asked Alec.

"Most of them. They have given me great pleasure."

"I don't have to read them all, do I?" Alec couldn't see how there would ever be time for anything else if he did.

"Well, maybe not all," laughed his grandfather. "But as many as you can. It's going to take a lot of self-discipline, Alec, but you can do it."

Later, in his room, Alec complained to Belle. "Why do I need to read all these books?" he grumbled. "You said there are ideas all around us in the world."

"There are ideas in books too, Alec. You've got to keep your mind open to everything. You'll learn a lot, you'll see. And you'll enjoy it, too. Self-discipline, Alec, self-discipline," laughed Belle.

"Self-discipline… self-discipline," muttered Alec. "But I guess everybody is right. It is going to take a lot." They were right, of course. And they were right about something else. Alec's year with his grandfather was hard work, but it was fun, too.

At the end of the year, Alec's father came to take him home.

"Before we leave, I want you to meet someone, Alec." Alec was overjoyed when he learned it was a famous scientist.

While his father and the scientist talked, Alec explored the scientist's workroom. In a corner, he found a machine built to look like a human head. Of course, he had to find out what it was. "What is this?" he asked the scientist.

"That's a talking head. I made it many years ago to show how we use our tongue and lips to help us talk. Watch this."

The scientist blew into a tube in the back of the machine and moved the lips. And do you know what happened next? The machine talked.

When they got back home, Mr. Bell challenged Alec and his older brother, Melville, to make their own talking machine. The brothers worked on it every spare minute.

Sometimes Melville would get discouraged. "We'll never get it to talk, Alec."

"Oh yes we will. We just have to keep working at it. There's always something new we can try or a new way of putting what we have together."

One afternoon, as Melville blew into its voice box, the machine said "aaah."

"We did it!" whooped Alec. Belle clanged wildly with joy. "Take it easy, Belle," laughed Alec. "You can get pretty noisy at times." Belle calmed down. Alec tried moving the tongue and lips, and before long the machine said "mama" just like a baby. They knew it sounded real when a neighbor knocked at the door and asked if there was a baby crying. Belle and the boys laughed until they hurt.

"Congratulations, boys," said Mr. Bell, when he heard the machine talk. "Now I have another job for you. I need you to help me teach my alphabet for the deaf."

"How does it work, father?" asked Alec. His work on the machine had made him very interested in speech and sound.

"We learn to speak by listening to people," explained Mr. Bell. "Those who are born deaf can't do that, so I've drawn pictures to show them how to hold their tongue and lips to make every sound of the English language. I call it Visible Speech.

"If you get discouraged because inventing takes so much self-discipline, Alec, just think how much a deaf person needs in order to learn to make sounds people can understand."

For the next few years Alec and Melville helped their father teach Visible Speech and give lectures about it to other teachers and scientists.

Sitting alone with Belle one day, Alec said sadly, "Mother is becoming deaf."

"Yes I know," replied Belle. "She must feel very cut off from the family, not being able to hear."

"I am sure she does. But, you know, Belle, in a way she's lucky. At least she knows how to speak. How much more lonely it must be for people who were born deaf and who have never learned to speak!"

As Alec got more involved with teaching the deaf to speak, he became fascinated with the question of how sound travels. He started doing experiments and enrolled at the university to learn more.

While Alec was at the university, tragedy struck the Bell family. Alec's younger brother, who had always been frail, became sick and died of a disease called tuberculosis. A few short months later, his older brother, Melville, died of the same disease. In those days they did not have the wonderful medicines we have today to cure such illness.

21

One day, Alec's mother noticed that his cheeks were flushed and he was very tired. These were signs of the disease that had killed her other two sons. Mrs. Bell was very worried.

"There must be something we can do," she said to her husband.

"There is. We can take him to a healthier climate."

"But where?" she asked.

"Canada. I spent some time there many years ago when my health was poor. It did wonders for me. And we have friends in Paris, Ontario. They will help us get settled."

So, the decision was made. They were sad to leave, but they knew how important it was to Alec's health. Not long afterwards, Alec found himself with his parents on a ship heading for Canada.

Alec was on deck when the ship docked in Quebec City. There were people everywhere, unloading boxes and bags, waving to friends, and shouting—in French! The buildings around the docks were made of wood instead of bricks, like the ones in Edinburgh. "Everything looks and sounds so strange, Belle," said Alec.

"I know, and you will probably feel a little homesick for a while." Alec agreed, but decided he was not going to let it get the better of him.

The Bells found a house in Brantford, Ontario. It was a white house, with black trim. "Look, Belle," cried Alec. "What a wonderful big front porch. I am really going to like this." Belle smiled at Alec's enthusiasm.

The house was called Tutelo Heights. It was built on a hill and overlooked the Grand River, which wound through the valley below. Among the birch trees on the edge of the hill, Alec and Belle found a hollow spot where they could sit and gaze at the view.

"I'll bring some blankets and pillows out here," Alec told Belle. "It will be my dreaming place."

There, Alec read and dreamed away the summer days. By the time the chilly Canadian autumn chased him indoors, his health was much improved.

About that time, Alec's father went on a lecture tour of the United States. While he was in Boston, he explained his Visible Speech method of teaching deaf people to talk to the head of the school for the deaf. He returned with good news for Alec. The school wanted Alec to teach there.

"Do you think you're strong enough yet?" worried Mrs. Bell.

"Oh yes," Alec assured her. "I feel so much better. I'll be fine. I'll miss you, of course."

"Promise me you won't work too hard and will get lots of rest."

"I promise," said Alec.

"And I'll see that you keep that promise," Belle warned Alec later. "An inventor may need to work and have self-discipline, but a healthy body is important too."

When he got to Boston, Alec went straight to the telegraph office to let his parents know he'd arrived safely. "I'm sorry, sir," the telegraph operator said, "but you'll have to wait. Someone else must be sending a message."

"Do you mean only one message can go along the wire at a time?"

"That's right. I can't send yours until the line is free."

That started Alec thinking. "Belle, there should be a way to send more than one telegraph message at a time. Perhaps I can figure out how to do it."

"You probably can," replied his friend. "But it won't be easy. You don't know very much about electricity, so you'll have a lot to learn."

Alec thought about the problem every spare minute. He attended lectures that he thought might help him and read all the books he could find on electricity.

Much of his time, of course, was taken up with his classes at the school for the deaf. The school was in an old house in the heart of Boston. Although it was full of students, it was a very quiet place. The students had never learned to talk because they couldn't hear what words sounded like.

Using Visible Speech, Alec quickly taught even the youngest ones a few words. And it wasn't long before some of them were speaking whole sentences. Their parents were amazed and very grateful to Alec.

One of the most grateful parents was Mr. Thomas Sanders. His five-year-old son, Georgie, had been deaf since birth. He needed a lot of help, and Alec was teaching him privately. One day Mr. Sanders approached Alec. "I am delighted with what you have done for Georgie."

"It gives me great pleasure to see his progress, sir," replied Alec.

"I would like to do something for you in return," said the kindly man. "I know you are not earning much money. Would it help if I provided you with a place to stay?"

"Why, that would be wonderful, sir."

"It's settled then. You can move into my mother's house whenever you're ready."

It turned out to be a nice large house outside Boston. Mrs. Sanders let Alec use the basement for his experiments.

Soon there were wires everywhere. They were strung from wall to wall, from the desk to the windows—just about anywhere they could be attached. In piles between the wires were books and all sorts of bits and pieces of equipment.

One day Mrs. Sanders came down to see how Alec was doing. She could hardly get in the door because of the wires and piles of books. "Oh my," she said. "Alec, how can you ever find anything in here?"

"Well," grinned Alec, "it isn't always easy."

Mrs. Sanders shook her head. "You'd better use the attic too. There's lots of space up there and the light is better."

Alec spent every night in his workshop, tinkering with his experiments or reading. Some nights there would be a light in the workshop long after midnight.

"Alec, you'll wear yourself out if you keep this up," Belle scolded. "You teach all day and work half the night. Self-discipline can include resting when that's what is best for you, you know, even if you'd rather keep working."

"I know, Belle, and I'll go to bed soon. But I am getting close to solving the problem. I can't stop now. Maybe if I try . . . ." And back Alec turned to his experiments.

Belle sighed. "I'm sure glad summer holidays are coming. You need a rest whether you think so or not."

Just before Alec went home to Brantford for the summer, a man came to see him with his deaf daughter. "This is my daughter, Mabel Hubbard," he said, introducing the young woman. "Mabel was able to hear and speak until she was four. Then she lost her hearing, and by now she has forgotten how words sound. She wants to learn to speak again."

Alec liked Mabel right away. Although she couldn't talk, her sparkling eyes said a lot. They told him she was a very smart and enthusiastic young lady.

Alec also liked Mabel's father. He told Mr. Hubbard about his experiments on the telegraph. Mr. Hubbard was a smart businessman and was very interested.

"But, Alec, how can you teach and experiment at the same time?" he asked.

Alec looked at Mabel. "I love teaching, sir," he said to her father. "And I consider it very important work. I couldn't think of giving it up."

"Well, then you must have someone to help you with your experiments. Let me pay for a helper. After all, you will do something far greater for my daughter—you'll give her back her voice." And so the two men agreed. When Alec returned to Boston in the fall he would hire a helper at Mr. Hubbard's expense.

Alec spent a relaxing summer at Brantford. He read and dreamed in his special dreaming place among the birch trees and dozed off listening to the wind rustle the summer leaves.

But even while he was dreaming, Alec's mind was at work. One lazy afternoon, as the crickets buzzed and the butterflies sunned themselves, Alec told Belle his latest idea.

"If we can send code messages over telegraph wires, why not voices?"

"Sometimes the things you think of surprise even me, Alec," replied Belle. "It's a wonderful idea."

It was such a wonderful idea that Alec couldn't get it out of his mind. He started working on it as soon as he got back to Boston. Now he was teaching at Boston University, as well as tutoring deaf students during the day and working on his inventions at night. More than ever, he needed a helper.

One day he wandered into a shop to buy some more wire and equipment for his experiments. It was a crowded, dirty and very noisy place. Off in the corner, a young man sat hunched over his work, as if he were all alone. He didn't seem to hear the noise of the hammers pounding or see the confusion around him. Alec asked the shop owner if he could speak to the young man.

"Mr. Watson," called the shop owner. The young man didn't even look up.

"That's the helper for me," Alec whispered to Belle. "Anyone who is so self-disciplined he can ignore the mess and the noise in this place won't have any trouble in my workshop."

Alec was right. Watson was a hard worker, who concentrated so completely on what he was doing that he forgot everything around him. And Alec discovered that Watson was a brilliant mechanic. No matter what piece of equipment Alec needed, Watson could make it for him.

Now that he had a helper, Alec had more time for his lessons with deaf students.

The lessons that he looked forward to most were Mabel Hubbard's. Mabel was a very quick learner, and soon she and Alec were having long talks. Mabel would speak slowly, and then she would watch Alec's lips as he spoke. They talked about many things. One day Alec told her about his idea for a telephone. "Wouldn't it be wonderful if I could really manage to send voices over a wire?"

Mabel smiled. In his enthusiasm, Alec had forgotten that, even if he succeeded, Mabel would never hear the voices. "It would be marvelous," Mabel said simply. She could understand that it really would be, for people who could hear. Besides, anything that Alec cared so much about was important to her.

A few days later, Alec and Watson tried their first experiment. They strung a wire from Alec's workshop out the window and into the living room of the house next door. Then they connected the wire to the neighbor's piano.

Alec went back up to his attic workshop, and Watson started to play the piano. Alec held a cup-shaped receiver at the end of the wire to his ear.

Could he hear sounds? Yes, he could. He could! Almost jumping for joy, Alec put down the receiver. Then his heart sank.

He still heard the sounds. The music had come through the open window between the houses, not over the wire.

"Our experiment failed, Belle," Alec said glumly.

"That's too bad, Alec. But don't be downhearted. Remember when you and Melville were working on your talking machine?" Alec nodded. But he was still feeling too disappointed to answer his friend.

"It took you a long time," Belle continued, "but with lots of self-discipline and hard work you made the machine talk."

"You're right, Belle," replied Alec. "There has to be a way to send sounds over a wire, and Watson and I are going to find it."

"That's the spirit, Alec."

Alec and Watson worked hard on their telephone experiments for
many months. Oh yes, it took self-discipline, but they made progress.

Meanwhile, Alec spent as much time as he could with Mabel Hubbard.

"You know, Alec, I think you are falling in love with that young
woman," laughed Belle one day.

"I think you may be right, Belle, as usual," replied Alec softly.

Mabel was in love with Alec, too. She was also very worried about him.

"You've got to stop being such a night-owl, Alec," she kept saying.

"I will, I will. But I work best at night. Maybe once I've solved this problem . . ."

But there was always some new problem. No matter how long or how hard Alec and Watson worked, nothing seemed to go right.

"You're tired, Alec," said Mabel. "You need a holiday. Go home to Brantford for a while. You know your time there always refreshes you. But before you go, I have a present for you. I've been painting your portrait. I'll send it over tomorrow."

Alec was packing his suitcase when the parcel was delivered. He opened it and burst out laughing. Mabel's portrait of him was a painting of a great white owl.

In Brantford, Alec tried to forget about the telephone as he lay resting in his favorite spot on the hill. Below him he could see the Grand River, and he could hear the excited voices of children playing on the bank. He thought about how their voices traveled through the air. Suddenly he had an idea of how to send voices over a telephone wire.

He was so excited he couldn't wait to get back to his Boston workshop. "I know it will work, Belle. I just know it."

Back in Boston, Alec sent for Watson immediately. He explained his idea, and they started to work again that very night.

The next afternoon they strung a wire from the workshop to the spare room next door. Then Watson talked into the mouthpiece in the spare room while Alec listened in the workshop. Alec thought he could hear Watson's voice over the wire, but no matter how hard he listened, he couldn't make out any words. All he could hear was a distant mumble.

It was progress, though. Belle jumped around in a frenzy of excitement. "Do be quiet, Belle," said Alec rather sharply. Belle looked crestfallen.

"I'm sorry," Alec said. "But you're making it hard for me to hear."

"I'll try to restrain myself from now on," apologized Belle. "I guess even I need a little self-discipline." Alec laughed and agreed.

Then one March day something wonderful happened. It was Alec's turn to shut himself in the spare room next door to the workshop and speak into the telephone.

Alec was about to sit down at the table that held the telephone when he had an accident. His elbow hit a battery that was sitting on the edge of the desk. It toppled over. Battery acid spilled onto his pants. It was so strong that it burned through his pants and started to sting his skin.

"Mr. Watson, come here. I want to see you," Alec cried into the telephone mouthpiece.

Seconds later, a red-faced excited Watson flung the door open. "I heard every word you said," he panted.

The first telephone call had been made! Alec was so happy he forgot about the acid and his stinging leg.

"There is still a lot to be done," Alec explained to Mabel later. "The telephone works between rooms that are next door to each other, but to be really useful it will have to carry voices much farther than that."

One day a few months later, the school for the deaf had a royal visitor. It was Dom Pedro, the emperor of Brazil. Dom Pedro wanted to start a similar school in his own country. He asked Alec many questions about Visible Speech and was very impressed by this young teacher who seemed so bright and so dedicated.

Alec didn't tell Dom Pedro about his inventions. In fact only the Hubbards and a few of his closest friends knew about the telephone.

"Alec, it's time you let the world know about your invention," said Mabel one day. "Why don't you take it to the Centennial Exhibition in Philadelphia and enter the science contest?"

"I think it's too late," answered Alec.

"Maybe my father can arrange it," suggested Mabel.

And sure enough, Mr. Hubbard did.

The Exhibition was a huge affair, spread over several buildings. One large hall was entirely filled with the latest scientific discoveries. Since Alec had registered late, he was given only a small, out-of-the-way corner of the hall to display his invention.

By late afternoon, the science contest judges were hot and tired. They wanted to stop before they had even seen Alec's invention. But one of the judges insisted they take the time to see it.

Can you guess who it was?

It was Dom Pedro. He had recognized Alec and felt sure that whatever this bright young man was showing would be worth seeing.

"I didn't know you would be here, Mr. Bell," Dom Pedro said.

"I've come to show my invention," replied Alec, "I call it the telephone."

"Then we must look at it," said the emperor.

When Alec and Watson demonstrated how the telephone worked, the judges were astounded. Each one wanted a turn at listening and speaking into Alec's invention. "This is really amazing," they exclaimed. "Think of the hard work and self-discipline it must have taken."

They all agreed to give Alec first prize.

Alec had discussed his telephone idea with his parents when he had first thought of it in Brantford. He had written to them often about his progress, and Mr. and Mrs. Bell were very eager to see how it worked. So, after the exhibition, Alec took his telephone home to Brantford.

When he got there, he discovered that his friends and neighbors had also heard about his amazing invention. So many came to visit the day he arrived that the house seemed ready to burst. Everyone hoped to see the telephone and try it.

"That Alec always was a special young man," said one neighbor. "Always asking questions," said another. "I've never known anyone with so much self-discipline," said a third.

Alec couldn't demonstrate his telephone for each person, one at a time. It would take too long. Finally he decided to try to send voices over the telegraph wire strung between Brantford and the town of Mount Pleasant, five miles away. He invited everyone to gather in the general store in Mount Pleasant to see how his telephone worked.

The night he made the call, the general store was filled with people. It was like a party, with everyone talking at once. Then, Alec asked everybody to be quiet, and he held the telephone receiver to his ear. The crowd watched his face and saw him smile. Alec could hear voices coming all the way from Brantford.

The crowd cheered and then people took turns listening. To their amazement, they not only heard voices, they understood the words spoken.

A few days later, Alec arranged for a telephone call between Brantford and Paris, Ontario, eight miles away. That call would go down in history as the world's first long distance phone call.

Back in Boston in the fall, Alec successfully made calls between towns many miles apart. Years later, he would also make the first transcontinental telephone call.

The telephone company arranged to have Watson waiting in San Francisco, and in New York, Alec repeated the first words ever spoken on the telephone: "Mr. Watson, come here, I want to see you."

Watson remarked that it would take rather longer this time.

A year after Alec's triumph in Philadelphia, Alec and Mabel were married. They traveled to England, where Alec opened a school for the deaf and demonstrated his telephone to Queen Victoria. The queen praised Alec's achievement. "If more people had your self-discipline, Mr. Bell, just think of what we could accomplish in this world."

Other honors flowed in. The French government gave him the famous Volta Prize, which had been awarded only a few times before. Alec used the prize money to build a laboratory. For you see, Alec's disciplined and searching mind was already thinking of many new ideas and ways of applying them.

Over the next few years Alec worked long and hard on several new inventions. And he continued to lecture to teachers of the deaf and help families with deaf children.

One day, a man brought his blind and deaf daughter to see Alec. Her name was Helen Keller, and her father was desperate. It seemed impossible to teach her anything.

Alec took her on his knee and watched her as she felt his watch strike the hour. He was sure she could be educated.

Since he himself had no experience teaching someone who was blind as well as deaf, Alec directed Mr. Keller to a school that might be able to help Helen. Through the school, the Kellers found Annie Sullivan, who taught Helen to "hear" and "talk" and "see" with her hands.

Alec followed Helen's progress, helping and encouraging her whenever he could. The two became life-long friends and Helen later said that without him she would have been locked in darkness and silence forever.

Meanwhile, Mabel was once again worrying about Alec's health. "You need a quiet place to rest sometimes," she told him. Alec's trusted little friend Belle chimed her agreement. And one summer, when they were visiting Nova Scotia, they found the perfect place.

It was near Baddeck on Cape Breton Island. Standing on a grassy hill that led down to a lake, Alec said to Mabel, "It reminds me of Scotland where I lived when I was a boy. We will build a summer place here and call it Beinn Bhreagh. That's Gaelic for 'beautiful mountain'."

Summers at Beinn Bhreagh did not mean just rest for Alec.
He built a small workshop attached to the house so that he could
do experiments. "Do you always have to work so hard and be so
self-disciplined?" asked Belle. Alec smiled. Belle knew he could not
be happy unless he was thinking up new ways of helping people.

Watching the birds circle overhead, Alec pondered the question of
how it might be possible for people to fly, too. He began experimenting
with kites, building ever bigger and more complicated ones.

In 1906, four eager, young men excited by the possibilities of flight found their way to Baddeck. One evening, as they all sat talking in the Bell living room, Mabel made a suggestion. "Alec, you have four pretty smart young engineers here, and they're just as interested in flight as you are. Why don't we form an organization?"

And that is just what they did.

They built and flew passenger-carrying kites, then moved on to gliders and finally to powered aircraft. On February 23, 1909, their *Silver Dart* flew half a mile at a speed of forty miles per hour. It was the first heavier-than-air flight in the British Empire.

Over the years, Alec's self-disciplined and enquiring mind took him from one invention to the next. It led him from kites and planes to boats to machines that could locate icebergs and take salt out of the sea water. He experimented with new breeds of sheep, wax phonograph records and air conditioning. He even invented a device by which doctors could locate a bullet or other metal object in the body.

But one of the inventions that pleased Alec the most was his machine that tested people's hearing. He hoped that by using it, doctors could identify hearing problems and treat them before they became serious.

Alec was honored with many awards for his inventions. Perhaps the honor that meant the most to him was having a Chicago school for deaf children named after him. For while we think of Alexander Graham Bell as a great inventor, he himself believed that his most important work was teaching the deaf how to speak.

Alexander Graham Bell never stopped asking questions about the world and following where the answers led him.

When he was asked to describe what an inventor does, he said:

> "The inventor is a man who looks upon the world and is not content with things as they are. He wants to improve whatever he sees, he wants to benefit the world, he is haunted by an idea."

Because Alexander Graham Bell had the self-discipline to keep searching and working and trying, the ideas that haunted him led to some of the greatest inventions of his time.

Not all of you can become world famous inventors. But if you have the self-discipline to keep working to improve whatever you see, as Alexander Graham Bell did, you might find you can do more than you had ever imagined possible.

The End

ALEXANDER GRAHAM BELL
1847-1922

Alexander Graham Bell liked to think of himself as, above all, a teacher of the deaf. However, to most people, he is known mainly as the inventor of the telephone. Actually, his contributions ranged far wider. Bell applied his inventive genius to an amazing variety of problems, and some of his ideas are still being developed today.

Alec was born in Edinburgh, Scotland, on March 3, 1847, the second of three children. His mother was a portrait painter and, in spite of growing deafness, an accomplished pianist. Both his father and his grandfather were well-known teachers of correct speech. His father was especially concerned about the problems of people who were born deaf and had developed a system called Visible Speech for teaching them to speak.

In his early years, Alec, like his two brothers, was taught at home. After five years of formal schooling, Alec was sent, at the age of 15, to spend a year with his grandfather in London. There he read a great deal and became particularly interested in speech and sound. He would later call this year a turning point in his life.

At the age of 16, Alec began teaching music and speech at a boys' school. In 1865 his parents moved to London, and he soon followed to assist his father in teaching Visible Speech to deaf children. During these years, Alec took courses at university and began experimenting on his own.

About this time, Alec's two brothers died of tuberculosis within a few months of each other. With Alec himself showing signs of the disease, his worried parents decided to seek a healthier climate in Canada.

The Bells settled in Brantford, Ontario, and Alec's health improved rapidly. In 1871 he was well enough to accept a job teaching Visible Speech at a school for the deaf in Boston. Then, from 1873 to 1877, he taught vocal physiology at Boston University. In his spare time, he continued studying and experimenting. By now he was interested in electricity and was working on a "harmonic telegraph," a system by which several messages could be carried over a wire at the same time. Eventually Alec's work on the telegraph would lead him to the idea of the telephone—an idea that came to him one summer in Brantford, where he had returned to spend his holidays.

Experiments cost money, however, and Alec had very little. Fortunately, two wealthy men, Gardiner Hubbard and Thomas Sanders, both parents of Alec's students, offered to give him financial support. Their help enabled him to hire an assistant, Thomas Watson, whose mechanical skills were matched only by his enthusiasm.

For two years, Alec, with Watson's help, worked hard on his experiments, concentrating more and more on the telephone. On March 7, 1876, a United States patent for "Improvements in Telegraphy," was taken out, and thereby the famous patent, number 174 465, was secured on the telephone. Three days later, on March 10, the first sentence was clearly transmitted: "Mr. Watson, come here. I want to see you." The telephone was born.

One of his students was Mabel Hubbard. She was the daughter of Gardiner Hubbard and had been deaf since the age of four as a result of scarlet fever. In 1877, she and Alec were married and they had two daughters and a long, happy, life together.

In 1885, Alec and Mabel bought property on Cape Breton Island in Nova Scotia. There they built a summer home they called Beinn Bhreagh, and there Alec conducted many of his most interesting experiments in fields ranging from sheep breeding to the sending of sound by light waves. With a group of young engineers he formed the Aerial Experiment Association which performed some of the most successful early experiments in flight. Their *Silver Dart* was the first heavier-than-air flight in the British Empire. His work in many areas opened the way for later inventions such as the electric eye, film sound tracks and the hydrofoil. Besides his teaching and inventions he was a founding member and President of the National Geographic Society.

Alexander Graham Bell's inventions brought him many honors, but he remained modest and generous and always maintained that teaching the deaf was his most important work.

Bell died on August 2, 1922 at Baddeck. So great was the respect he had earned that during his funeral all the telephones in North America were silent in his honor.

The ValueTale Series